EVERY DAY
IS A FRESH
BEGINNING

EVERY DAY IS A FRESH BEGINNING

Meaningful Poems for Life

Chosen by

AOIBHÍN GARRIHY

eriu

First published in 2022 by Eriu
an imprint of Bonnier Books UK
4th Floor, Victoria House
Bloomsbury Square
London, WC1B 4DA

A CIP catalogue record for this book is available from the British Library.

Hardback ISBN: 978-1-80418-081-5

Also available as an ebook and an audiobook

3 5 7 9 10 8 6 4 2

Typeset in Bodoni by Envy Design Ltd
Printed and bound in Great Britain by Clays Ltd, Elcograf S.p.A.

Eriu is an imprint of Bonnier Books UK
www.bonnierbooks.co.uk

For Mom and Dad with all my love x

Contents

Introduction

POETRY IS LANGUAGE AT ITS MOST DISTILLED
AND MOST POWERFUL

Rita Dove

Poetry has always been a constant in my life. During the milestones, the big moments, poetry seemed to mark each and every one. But it was also there in the quieter times, a form of solace and a path to meditation, bringing me comfort and inspiration when I needed it most. It always featured to such a degree that I almost took it for granted and forgot the power it holds for me.

It took a few turbulent years and a global pandemic for me to realise how much I truly valued the healing power of words. I found myself turning to poetry more and more when I felt confused, angry, overwhelmed, sad but also elated, overjoyed and totally in love. I was drawn to the words of others and sometimes even felt compelled to write myself, however simply.

Perhaps poetry requires you to be in a certain headspace. Lockdown gave us that time, that headspace and the spark was reignited for me and so many others, it seems.

In 2020 I took to my wardrobe (it was the closest thing to a sound recording booth!) and began to read, recite, record and share some poems that had a deep meaning for me, and it was possibly my biggest awakening over the past few years. I recently heard Ethan Hawke speak about poetry and art and how in our hour of need, it's no longer a luxury; it's sustenance. We need it. This was certainly true for me.

Now, I keep my poetry books by my bed and at the end of the day, depending on my mood or what's going on that day, I scan those books for that sustenance, a poem, some healing words to help me process a particular emotion or feeling. That for me is therapy.

My love for poetry began with my dad. He left school at sixteen but that didn't stop his poetic flair – a great man to put pen to paper should the mood take him. He wrote four rhyming stanzas titled 'Aoibhín O Aoibhín' on the back of a cigarette box while I was watching from the buggy on a lazy sunny afternoon! The poem detailed the delightful nappy-changing cycle and it still hangs proudly in Mom and Dad's downstairs loo. It didn't make the final cut for this anthology, needless to say, but I'm delighted one of his more recent works does!

I think for most of us, our relationship with poetry began with our teachers. I was lucky enough to have wonderful teachers who instilled a love and appetite for poems and poetry recitation in me from a very early age. I remember learning and reciting my very first poem at the school *feis*, 'Queen Bee' by Mary K. Robinson. I still remember every line:

When I was in the garden,
I saw a great Queen Bee:
She was the very largest one
That I did ever see.
She wore a shiny helmet
And a lovely velvet gown,
But I was rather sad, because
She didn't wear a crown!

In second class I had a very special teacher, Miss Susan Ryan. One of those teachers who leaves a lasting impression on you, forever etched in your heart. I was besotted with her. We all were. She was larger than life and loved the arts. So theatrical, full of charisma and when it came to poetry, the words jumped off the page when Miss Ryan would recite. She would animate every line in a way I will never forget.

I had a truly wonderful Speech and Drama teacher,

Maeve O'Donoghue, growing up and throughout my teenage years in particular she honed and developed my love, knowledge and appreciation for poetry, the language and the power of the voice. It was the extracurricular activity that took me away from the pressures of study and school life. I loved to play with the delivery, the musicality of the vowels and consonants, the rhyme and rhythm, the inflection, the expression in the voice and in the face to engage and tell the story and capture the emotion through this very unique medium.

That passion was solidified further when I went to Trinity College Dublin and began my Bachelor in Acting Studies course at the Samuel Beckett Theatre. Voice Coach Andrea Ainsworth would spend hours dissecting every verse, line, word, syllable and I felt so privileged to have had that time and space to indulge. That was a special time in my life – I was in a bubble, playing, honing, telling, sharing, trying, failing, trying again without the pressure of the industry and the reality of being a jobbing actor!

It wasn't until I taught Speech and Drama myself later on and began to share and explore poetry with my own young students, making new discoveries through their eyes, that I developed a deeper appreciation of the form and discovered how, regardless of the century, certain themes are universal and totally timeless.

And so this poetry anthology feels like the most natural, joyous project I have ever embarked on. I felt like I was back in the dance studio of the Samuel Beckett Theatre 'indulging'! But I want you to indulge with me. I have shared some thoughts on each of the choices but have also left room for yours. Poetry is subjective and open to each individual interpretation, which has always been the beauty of it. The poems reflect big and small moments in the journeys of our lives, from our dreams and our relationships to love and loss, courage and compassion.

I wanted to break down the barrier some might have to poetry; to create an accessible collection of poems you really don't need a degree in English to enjoy. I wanted to encourage a love for this special form. I really wanted to share some of my favourites; the poems that resonated for me at different points in my life and helped to bring comfort. I wanted to share poems that inspire, poems that empathise, poems that encourage us all to pause, but also to persevere. Poems that bring hope for tomorrow…because every day really is a fresh beginning.

The hope and optimism in this poem have helped me through the toughest days. It's a beautiful reminder that this too shall pass, and every day is a new opportunity to begin again.

New Every Morning

Susan Coolidge

Every morn is the world made new.
You who are weary of sorrow and sinning,
Here is a beautiful hope for you, –
A hope for me and a hope for you.

All the past things are past and over;
The tasks are done and the tears are shed.
Yesterday's errors let yesterday cover;
Yesterday's wounds, which smarted and bled,
Are healed with the healing which night has shed.

Yesterday now is a part of forever,
Bound up in a sheaf, which God holds tight,
With glad days, and sad days, and bad days,
    which never
Shall visit us more with their bloom and their blight,
Their fulness of sunshine or sorrowful night.

Let them go, since we cannot re-live them,
Cannot undo and cannot atone;
God in his mercy receive, forgive them!
Only the new days are our own;
To-day is ours, and to-day alone.

Here are the skies all burnished brightly,
Here is the spent earth all re-born,
Here are the tired limbs springing lightly
To face the sun and to share with the morn
In the chrism of dew and the cool of dawn.

Every day is a fresh beginning;
Listen, my soul, to the glad refrain,
And, spite of old sorrow and older sinning,
And puzzles forecasted and possible pain,
Take heart with the day, and begin again.

The resilience of people in the face of adversity never ceases to amaze me. How some people continue to pick themselves up and dust themselves off is incredible. This poem is a reminder of that determination, that innate human ability to start again anew.

Begin

Brendan Kennelly

Begin again to the summoning birds
to the sight of light at the window,
begin to the roar of morning traffic
all along Pembroke Road.
Every beginning is a promise
born in light and dying in dark
determination and exaltation of springtime
flowering the way to work.
Begin to the pageant of queuing girls
the arrogant loneliness of swans in the canal
bridges linking the past and future
old friends passing though with us still.
Begin to the loneliness that cannot end
since it perhaps is what makes us begin,
begin to wonder at unknown faces
at crying birds in the sudden rain
at branches stark in the willing sunlight
at seagulls foraging for bread
at couples sharing a sunny secret
alone together while making good.
Though we live in a world that dreams of ending
that always seems about to give in
something that will not acknowledge conclusion
insists that we forever begin.

I discovered Morgan Harper Nichols's work on social media and she's one of those people who provides the type of content you love to read and reread and share. This poem is one of my favourites from her beautiful book of the same title. It's a reminder that sometimes struggle is necessary for growth and when you are faced with adversity you discover what it is you are truly made of.

All Along You Were Blooming

Morgan Harper Nichols

And the thing about blooming is,
nothing about the process is easy.
It requires every part of you to
stretch upward, with your roots
firmly planted in the ground; and
in the sun; and in the rain, and
wind, you stand anyway, even
against the pull of the soil. And
through it all, one day you will see
all along you were transforming.
This took everything out of you,
but the struggle was beautiful
and necessary for your growth.

I read this poem in peak lockdown, willing and wishing the weeks to pass. Amy's words reframed things in that instant for me – wishing for the future prevents us from appreciating the present. It's a great reminder to live in the moment.

Soon

Amy De Bhrún

Soon.
It'll all be different soon.
It'll all be better soon.
But soon isn't now
And now we are here.
Here we are.
Now.
This moment.
This breath.
It's the only certainty.
Hanging onto soon
Is the noose that will choke you.
Say hello to this moment
And breathe the deepest breath you can.
And soon
Will be the now you were so desperately waiting for.

Busy is often worn as a badge of honour to the detriment of our overall wellbeing. However, this is the type of busy I can absolutely get on board with!

I'm Busy

Brooke Hampton

I'm busy;
but not in the way
most people accept.
I'm busy calming my fear
and finding my courage.
I'm busy listening to my kids.
I'm busy getting in touch
with what is real.
I'm busy growing things and
connecting with the natural world.
I'm busy questioning my answers.
I'm busy being present in my life.

I came across this poem during a staycation in Dingle, Co. Kerry. I can honestly say it made the trip. As soon as I read it, I put the phone down, forgot about work, any reservations I had about taking some time out disappeared and I thoroughly enjoyed the break. It has now become my little holiday mantra.

Leisure

W.H. Davies

What is this life if, full of care,
We have no time to stand and stare?

No time to stand beneath the boughs,
And stare as long as sheep or cows.

No time to see, when woods we pass,
Where squirrels hide their nuts in grass.

No time to see, in broad daylight,
Streams full of stars, like skies at night.

No time to turn at Beauty's glance,
And watch her feet, how they can dance.

No time to wait till her mouth can
Enrich that smile her eyes began.

A poor life this if, full of care,
We have no time to stand and stare.

When I find myself overthinking, anxious or stressed I often turn to Mother Nature, and she generally has the answers. I love this poem for its peace and tranquillity.

The Peace of Wild Things

Wendell Berry

When despair for the world grows in me
and I wake in the night at the least sound
in fear of what my life and my children's lives may be,
I go and lie down where the wood drake
rests in his beauty on the water, and the great
    heron feeds.
I come into the peace of wild things
who do not tax their lives with forethought
of grief. I come into the presence of still water.
And I feel above me the day-blind stars
waiting with their light. For a time
I rest in the grace of the world, and am free.

When I read this poem, for some reason it brought me straight back to my Leaving Cert year, yearning for freedom and an open road. The moment I handed up my final paper, the world suddenly became my oyster!

Freedom

Olive Runner

Give me the long, straight road before me,
    A clear, cold day with a nipping air,
Tall, bare trees to run on beside me,
    A heart that is light and free from care.
Then let me go! – I care not whither
    My feet may lead, for my spirit shall be
Free as the brook that flows to the river,
    Free as the river that flows to the sea.

When I found this poem mid-lockdown, I felt that Francis had read my mind. I went for a solo walk in the woods that day, found a spot where the light was breaking through the branches, stopped and placed my hand on the trunk of a tree and stayed there for a while as a sense of calm came over me. While I always appreciated the healing power of nature, I had never done anything like that before. That day I felt a special connection to Mother Earth, and it was indeed a blessing.

Blessings

Francis Harvey

Yesterday, for some reason I couldn't
understand, I suddenly felt starved of
trees and had to make tracks towards
the beeches of Lough Eske to set my heart
at ease and stand there slowly adjusting
myself to the overwhelming presence of all
those trees. It was like coming back among
people again after living for ages
alone and as I reached out and laid my
right hand in blessing on the trunk of
a beech that had the solidity but not
the coldness of stone I knew it for
the living thing it was under the palm
of my hand as surely as I know the living
sensuousness of flesh and bone and my
blessing was returned a hundredfold
before it was time for me to go home.

We all enter and exit this world the very same way and we have much more in common than we think.

Common Things

Ann Hawkshaw

The sunshine is a glorious thing,
    That comes alike to all;
Lighting the peasant's lowly cot,
    The noble's painted hall.

The moonlight is a gentle thing,
    It through the window gleams
Upon the snowy pillow where
    The happy infant dreams.

It shines upon the fisher's boat
    Out on the lovely sea,
Or where the little lambkins lie
    Beneath the old oak-tree.

The dew-drops on the summer morn
    Sparkle upon the grass;
The village children brush them off
    That through the meadows pass.

There are no gems in monarch's crowns
    More beautiful than they;
And yet we scarcely notice them,
    But tread them off in play.

Poor Robin on the pear-tree sings
  Beside the cottage-door;
The heath-flower fills the air with sweets,
  Upon the pathless moor.

There are as many lovely things,
  As many pleasant tones,
For those who sit by cottage-hearths
  As those who sit on thrones!

This poem was written by the former American First Lady when she was just ten years of age. I taught it to my Speech and Drama students and thought, 'Jackie hit the nail on the head here.' As her husband, John F. Kennedy, later said, 'We are tied to the ocean. And when we go back to the sea, whether it is to sail or to watch it, we are going back from whence we came.'

Sea Joy

Jacqueline Bouvier

When I go down by the sandy shore
I can think of nothing I want more
Than to live by the booming blue sea
As the seagulls flutter round about me

I can run about – when the tide is out
With the wind and the sand and the sea all about
And the seagulls are swirling and diving for fish
Oh – to live by the sea is my only wish.

For the sea swimmers – 'We must have a turn together'. I love that idea of dancing with the ocean. All those good endorphins you get from dancing – the same could be said about the wondrous sea.

You Sea! *from* Song of Myself

Walt Whitman

You sea! I resign myself to you also – I guess what
    you mean,
I behold from the beach your crooked inviting fingers,
I believe you refuse to go back without feeling of me,
We must have a turn together, I undress, hurry me out
    of sight of the land,
Cushion me soft, rock me in billowy drowse,
Dash me with amorous wet, I can repay you.

Sea of stretch'd ground-swells,
Sea breathing broad and convulsive breaths,
Sea of the brine of life and of unshovell'd yet always-
    ready graves,
Howler and scooper of storms, capricious and dainty
    sea,
I am integral with you, I too am of one phase and of
    all phases.

I discovered Anne Casey when compiling this anthology and the discovery was the highlight of this project for me. Her work, in particular her own recitations and introductions online, moved me to tears. Hailing from West Clare, Anne is inspired by her home place and the result is magic.

I will arise and go

(*After William Butler Yeats*)

Anne Casey

My people are a migrant clan
Prospering not by hook or crook or craft
But by diligent labour and an easy charm
Flung from one small corner
Across every wind-tossed sea
Mountaintop to valley floor
To lay a thousand roadways
Or stand on pavements grey
To explore wild tropical outposts
Hold fast to frozen plains

My people are an itinerant tribe
A heathen spirit tamed
Not by bonds or shackles or shekels
But by music and by elegant words
Though alongside our wanderlust
Cohabits a want in us –
That surges in each nomad breast –
To journey back again, top the last crest
To that first wide view
Across a childhood shore

To feel the heart leap
Like a salmon returned to familial waters
If only – in our dreams

This poem stands out from schooldays. I had a passionate English teacher who delivered it with feeling! I think it's a great reminder of how we all have a responsibility on this earth and an obligation to play our part, particularly in today's world.

'No man is an island'

John Donne

No man is an island,
Entire of itself;
Every man is a piece of the continent,
A part of the main;
If a clod be washed away by the sea,
Europe is the less,
As well as if a promontory were,
As well as if a manor of thy friend's
Or of thine own were;
Any man's death diminishes me,
Because I am involved in mankind;
And therefore never send to know
For whom the bell tolls;
It tolls for thee.

If you have a friend or a friendship like the one depicted here by Sean Brophy, it's safe to say you are very lucky. I read this having not seen my sisters (my best friends) in a long time and I instantly thought of them. I feel so lucky to say every word is true.

Friendship

Sean Brophy

When I think of friends
I think of easy company
Of no masks, ever

I think of shared experience,
That binds together

I think of judgement suspended
I think of understanding
Of walking in each other's shoes

I think of acceptance
Of what we are
I think of belief in what we try to be
In authenticity

I think of you and you and you
My friends,
My dear friends

I think of you.

More recently, when the insecurity of teenage years left us and we set out on our various paths in life, our mom adopted a new title for herself, our 'frank friend without a filter'. She said she would be failing in her duty if she did not deliver the hard truth when required. This one is for her and anyone who tells it like it is!

Friendship

Dinah Maria Mulock Craik

Oh, the comfort – the inexpressible
    comfort of feeling safe with a person,
  Having neither to weigh thoughts,
Nor measure words – but pouring them
  All right out – just as they are –
Chaff and grain together –
  Certain that a faithful hand will
Take and sift them –
  Keep what is worth keeping –
And with the breath of kindness
  Blow the rest away.

I remember watching a Ted Talk with Jane Fonda and she said, 'Women's friendships are a renewable source of power' and how we rarely see that depicted in the media, women loving and caring for one another – I think this poem beautifully depicts the importance of friends old and new.

New Friends and Old Friends

Joseph Parry

Make new friends, but keep the old
Those are silver, these are gold
New-made friendships, like new wine
Age will mellow and refine
Friendships that have stood the test
Of time and change – are surely best
Brow may wrinkle, hair grow gray
Friendship never knows decay
For 'mid old friends, tried and true
Once more we reach and youth renew
But old friends, alas, may die
New friends must their place supply
Cherish friendships in your breast
New is good, but old is best
Make new friends, but keep the old
Those are silver, these are gold

This poem reminds me of the Nicholas Sparks novel and movie The Notebook. Ever the romantic, I count it one of my favourites. Similarly, I think this beautiful poem by Gabriel Fitzmaurice depicts a maturing love, a deep understanding and an ease in one another's company – the comfort of companionship.

Just To Be Beside You Is Enough

Gabriel Fitzmaurice

Just to be beside you is enough,
Just to make your breakfast tea and toast,
To help you with the ware, that kind of stuff,
Just to get the papers and your post;
To hold you in my arms in calm embrace,
Just to sit beside you at the fire,
Just to trace my fingers on your face
Is more to me than all of youth's desire;
Just to lie beside you in the night,
To hear you breathe in peace before I sleep,
To wake beside you in the morning light
In the love we sowed together that we reap.
Together we have taken smooth and rough.
Just to be beside you is enough.

The last two lines of this poem could possibly be my favourite two lines of poetry ever written. The imagery but also the vulnerability in this famous love poem makes it truly endearing.

Aedh Wishes for the Cloths of Heaven

W.B. Yeats

Had I the heavens' embroidered cloths,
Enwrought with golden and silver light,
The blue and the dim and the dark cloths
Of night and light and the half light,
I would spread the cloths under your feet:
But I, being poor, have only my dreams;
I have spread my dreams under your feet;
Tread softly because you tread on my dreams.

Apart from being one of the most beautifully written love sonnets in the English language, I love that Elizabeth Barrett Browning's husband (whom the sonnet is about) was her biggest supporter and champion as a female poet in the nineteenth century, despite her tendency to outshine him in the literary stakes. It makes it all the more romantic.

Sonnet 43

Elizabeth Barrett Browning

How do I love thee? Let me count the ways.
　I love thee to the depth and breadth and height
　My soul can reach, when feeling out of sight
For the ends of Being and ideal Grace.
I love thee to the level of every day's
　Most quiet need, by sun and candlelight.
　I love thee freely, as men strive for Right.
I love thee purely, as they turn from Praise.
I love thee with the passion put to use
　In my old griefs, and with my childhood's faith.
I love thee with a love I seemed to lose
　With my lost saints – I love thee with the breath,
Smiles, tears, of all my life! – and, if God choose,
　I shall but love thee better after death.

It takes courage to fully lean into one's true and authentic self. Own that self-portrait.

Self-Portrait

David Whyte

It doesn't interest me if there is one God
or many gods.
I want to know if you belong or feel
abandoned.
If you know despair or can see it in others.
I want to know
if you are prepared to live in the world
with its harsh need
to change you. If you can look back
with firm eyes
saying this is where I stand. I want to know
if you know
how to melt into that fierce heat of living
falling toward
the center of your longing. I want to know
if you are willing
to live, day by day, with the consequence of love
and the bitter
unwanted passion of your sure defeat.

I have heard in that fierce embrace, even
the gods speak of God.

I had the privilege of reciting this poem at my sister Ailbhe and her husband Ruaidhri's wedding and I have loved it ever since.

Chapter One of One Thousand

O.J. Preston

For two people this dawn brought on a magical day
Now husband and wife they head on their way
As a boat setting sail may their journey begin
With calmest of waters, most helpful of wind
And if they should stumble upon turbulent sea
May it pass them unharming – leave them be.

For here are two people whom love has well bitten
Here opens their book which has yet to be written
As the first page unfolds and their life inks its path
May it write a true story where forever love lasts
Let their journey be happy till death do they part
Of one thousand chapters may this be the start.

This poem stopped me in my tracks. What a beautiful way to describe a relationship that may be past the initial 'honeymoon period'. The last line is my favourite.

A Decade

Amy Lowell

When you came, you were like red wine and honey,
And the taste of you burnt my mouth with its sweetness.
Now you are like morning bread,
Smooth and pleasant.
I hardly taste you at all for I know your savor,
But I am completely nourished.

When loves turns sour – we spent lots of time in college working on Shakespeare's love sonnets but this take on toxic love always interested me. Perhaps for its sheer passion. Of course, there are many beautiful, romantic works to choose from but when things are less than rosy, Sonnet 147!

Sonnet 147

William Shakespeare

My love is as a fever longing still
For that which longer nurseth the disease;
Feeding on that which doth preserve the ill,
The uncertain-sickly appetite to please.
My reason, the physician to my love,
Angry that his prescriptions are not kept,
Hath left me, and I desperate now approve,
Desire is death, which physic did except.
Past cure I am, now reason is past care,
And frantic-mad with evermore unrest:
My thoughts and my discourse as madmen's are,
At random from the truth vainly express'd;
    For I have sworn thee fair, and thought thee bright,
    Who art as black as hell, as dark as night.

It's an immense challenge to single out just one Heaney poem. This one hung in our kitchen at home growing up and always stayed with me – I love the reassuring nature of it. A gorgeous poem for newlyweds, perhaps a couple moving into a new home or anyone at all...

Scaffolding

Seamus Heaney

Masons, when they start upon a building,
Are careful to test out the scaffolding;

Make sure that planks won't slip at busy points,
Secure all ladders, tighten bolted joints.

And yet all this comes down when the job's done
Showing off walls of sure and solid stone.

So if, my dear, there sometimes seem to be
Old bridges breaking between you and me

Never fear. We may let the scaffolds fall
Confident that we have built our wall.

I think this poem by Steve Denehan is one of the most beautiful love poems I have ever read. Of course this is a big statement to make but something about that nostalgia moves me every single time I read it.

A Poem from My Father to My Mother

Steve Denehan

Remember when we met
when I was a kite
when you were the wind
when Dublin was dance-hall days
foggy nights
what-ifs and maybes
remember when I fell into myself
how you forgave me
and forgive me still
remember Burt Bacharach in the hotel lobby
when you exclaimed, 'It's him!'
remember how we used to dance
how the room spun with us
This Guy's in Love with You
remember when you said, 'Yes.'
remember those funhouse mirror years
when you remained a childless mother
remember the worry in your voice
when you threw the word into the air
not knowing if I would catch it
'Adoption…'
remember how I was the fool
who should have held you

more

remember how they grew
in our arms
on our laps
how they left
but never leave
remember when months became decades
and we forgave ourselves
for getting old
remember before
I started
to forget
remember when we ran across the dawn
or wanted to, at least

This is a very personal contribution. As I mentioned in my intro, Dad has been writing poems for us for years. This is a special one he wrote for my husband John and me on our wedding day. I loved it from the moment I read it and felt very proud to recite it that day. Anyone who knows the area of West/North Clare will appreciate the beautiful imagery and deep connection to the landscape. It's always been there for Dad and in turn has been passed on to me.

Doolin Romance

Eugene Garrihy

With my true love we gazed out,
on beauty out of dreams
Where lunar landscapes kiss the bogs
and gentians speckle greens.

He held my hand on Moher's edge,
Where streams and rivers flow
We watched the puffins break through shells
Revealing coloured glow.

He asked me if I'd be his bride
to love for ever more,
My answer pounding in my heart
You're the one that I adore.

Then gannets dived and salmon leaped
And dolphins danced at sea
A thousand birds of every hue
Sang sweet in harmony.

We tip toed oer those lunar slopes
On this ice created space
With floral carpet at our feet
On the Burren's woven lace.

And music flowed from every house
With roofs of straw and tile.
We danced all night on Moher flags
Then kissed by moonlight stile.

We strolled boreens to heather hills
With scents of mountain thyme
And viewed the church on distant hill
Where now our hands entwine.

A descendent of this place I am,
So someday we might share,
With children and their children too
This jewel in Co Clare.

During the pandemic this poem felt incredibly poignant. Human touch is the most natural, innate and comforting thing and all of a sudden it felt so alien. Here's a celebration of it...to remind ourselves.

Holding Hands

Michelle Yeo

At play, for fun
Here are kids just holding hands:
A natural handhold
That says 'I like you;'
Hands creamed with ice cream
Know only fun not stickiness.
In love, in despair,
Here behold the holding of hands:
A tender embrace,
Fingers locked in a twine;
A comforting squeeze of hands
That spells, 'I understand.'
At birth, at death,
Here we witness the holding of hands:
A baby's fingers
Clasping a mother's finger;
A hand all limp and lifeless
Lovingly held to a mourning cheek.
Holding hands is the language of man,
So profound yet simple;
Always touching, infinitely soothing,
Whatever life's precious moment:
At play, for fun
In love, in despair,
At birth, at death,
And all else in between.

'I'll be happy when...'

Perhaps we are all guilty of uttering these words at various stages of our lives. This poem reminds us that we are not defined by physical appearance, material things or indeed anything outside of our true authentic selves. A gentle reminder to always practise self-love and compassion, particularly when you feel the odds may be against you.

Not

Erin Hanson

You are not your age, nor the size of clothes you wear,
You are not a weight, or the color of your hair.
You are not your name, or the dimples in your cheeks.
You are all the books you read, and all the words
    you speak.
You are your croaky morning voice, and the smiles
    you try to hide.
You're the sweetness in your laughter, and every tear
    you've cried.
You're the songs you sing so loudly when you know
    you're all alone.
You're the places that you've been to, and the one
    that you call home.
You're the things that you believe in, and the people
    whom you love.
You're the photos in your bedroom, and the future
    you dream of.
You're made of so much beauty, but it seems that
    you forgot
When you decided that you were defined by all the
    things you're not.

They say the moment a child is born, the parent is also born. That first year is the most transformative year for any new parent. Karen McMillan gives a beautiful raw account of it in this piece, and it brings me instantly back.

That First Year

Karen McMillan

The year that two became three
No. More. Hot. Tea.

The year of not leaving your side
For more than an hour
And feeling revived
From a two minute shower

The year of white noise
Cuddles and baby slings
As you slowly adjust
To the outside things

The year of sleep regressions
Monkey impressions
Panicked Google searches
Too many to mention

The year I realised that women
Really do hold all the powers
Rocking and pacing
For hours and hours

Being more selective of
The company I keep
And dreading that question
So how does he sleep?

The year of building
All the rods for my own back
Binning the baby books
And not looking back

Endless walks with the pram
To help you to nap
Pounding the pavements
Looking like crap

One whole year to realise
That there's no wrong or right
There's what works
What you need
In the middle of the night

The year of doubts and fears
And bending the ears
Of family and friends
He'll sleep eventually
But when?

But you're more than
Your sleep struggles
So much more

You're that look of wonder
At a knock on the door
Your giggles
Your protests
And that tiny roar

Beaming with pride
As you take in your stride
Learning to roll, crawl and stand
And wave your wee hand

A sudden respect for those
Who've done all this before
But with two, with three, with four
Or more

The year of grand plans and dreams
Of these homemade cuisines
But some days just called
For eggs, chips and beans

And yet somehow you thrived
And we just about survived
The hourly wake-ups,
And some almost-breakups

You really did shake-up
These two kids

If poetry wasn't the best medicine, the innocence of a four-year-old surely would be. I have a little girl this very same age so naturally I think this Christopher Morley piece is just magic.

To A Child

Christopher Morley

The greatest poem ever known
Is one all poets have outgrown:
The poetry, innate, untold,
Of being only four years old.

Still young enough to be a part
Of Nature's great impulsive heart,
Born comrade of bird, beast, and tree
And unselfconscious as the bee –

And yet with lovely reason skilled
Each day new paradise to build;
Elate explorer of each sense,
Without dismay, without pretense!

In your unstained transparent eyes
There is no conscience, no surprise:
Life's queer conundrums you accept,
Your strange divinity still kept.

Being, that now absorbs you, all
Harmonious, unit, integral,
Will shred into perplexing bits, –
Oh, contradictions of the wits!

And Life, that sets all things in rhyme,
may make you poet, too, in time –
But there were days, O tender elf,
When you were Poetry itself!

This little Irish poem has a universal message. The days can be long, but the years are short. Cherish them.

Subh Milis

Seamus O Neill

Bhí subh milis
Ar bhaschrann an dorais
Ach mhúch mé an corraí
Ionam a d'éirigh,
Mar smaoinigh mé ar an lá
A bheas an baschrann glan,
Agus an lámh bheag
Ar iarraidh.

Jam

There was jam
On the door handle
But I suppressed the vexation
That rose up in me
Because I thought of the day
That the door handle would be clean
And the little hand
Would be gone.

I often get emotional when reading motherly musings. Maria Tempany documents so many of those moments of overwhelm, sheer joy, vulnerability, guilt, exhaustion and undeniable love so wonderfully. This particular one caught me off guard. It's a little reminder to us all, put the phone away, unplug and simply be.

Mama, Put the Phone Away

Maria Tempany

I got a rude awakening when
My son said to me today
With a look so earnest in his eyes
'Mama, put the phone away'

I was rooted to that very spot
When, yet again, he said
'Mama, put it down, right over there.
Come play with me instead.'

A sense of shame engulfed me.
And all at once I knew
How right he really truly was
Despite his ripe old age of two.

As instructed, down I got,
To play with my sweet boy.
To dissipate that shame I felt,
And replace it with pure joy.

What affirmations we may seek,
Behind these screens we all possess.
Can often be a source of pain,
Upset and much distress.

Did anybody like my post?
A follow? Or a share?
Quite frankly and perhaps he's right
My son really doesn't care.

Of course all these communities
Have an important role to play.
Especially in the times we're in
With those we love at bay.

But for me this simple statement
From the centre of my world.
Struck a cord so painfully
I felt compelled to share this word.

So, one and all, why don't we try
To 'put the phones away'.
Not all the time, just now and then.
And, ever present, try to stay.

There is no denying the beautiful imagery in Emily Brontë's work but I particularly love the final stanza in this piece for the hope and the reference to the sea, to which so many of us turn for solace.

Past, Present, Future

Emily Brontë

Tell me, tell me, smiling child,
What the past is like to thee?
'An Autumn evening soft and mild
With a wind that sighs mournfully.'

Tell me, what is the present hour?
'A green and flowery spray
Where a young bird sits gathering its power
To mount and fly away.'

And what is the future, happy one?
'A sea beneath a cloudless sun;
A mighty, glorious, dazzling sea
Stretching into infinity.'

I have enjoyed this poem with many of my students and it was the first poem I taught my girls. It's an easy poem for the little ones to remember but it also has a big message for us all.

The Little Elf Man

J.K. Bangs

I met a little elf man, once,
   Down where the lilies blow.
I asked him why he was so small,
   And, why he didn't grow.

He slightly frowned, and with his eye
   He looked me through and through.
'I'm just as big for me,' said he,
   'As you are big for you!'

A little farewell poem to our first home.

No. 32

Aoibhín Garrihy

As I lay in this bed for the very last time
Memories of a decade are flooding my mind
And this house that felt big in the early days
Became packed full of love in so many ways.

And before the pitter patter of feet or paws
It was just me and you and all of our flaws
These walls bore witness to some highs and some lows
'If they could speak...' as the saying goes.

We dreamt of this day, a labour of love,
A passion project, a gift from above
But now that it's here, a part of me sighs
Am I ready to leave this huge part of our lives?

A haven, a safe place where our family grew
We danced in the kitchen, we sang in the loo!
The place where suddenly I became we,
Woman turned Mom, two became three...

And now that it's time to say goodbye
There's an air of sadness for those days gone by
Precious times and memories made,
Thank you, house, for all that you gave.

I know it's the natural course of events
But I'll never forget this time that we spent
And if the next abode brings us half the luck
It'll be another great chapter in our life's book.

As the poet Denise Blake said herself about this poem, 'sometimes a soft lie is better than the brutal truth'.

And They All Lived Happily

Denise Blake

All the bad guys died in the end.
My kiss did make bruises better.
It was right to put lost teeth under a pillow
and that time, when you didn't find money,
there really was a tooth-fairy holiday.

I told the truth about castor oil
as you have grown big and strong.
Broccoli, porridge, the last bit on your plate,
have been the making of you.
I really believed your Granny would get better.
I didn't think your eyes would possibly stick
that way, but it seemed the thing to say.
That report card wasn't worth all my giving out,
I knew your teacher had a pick against you
but how to admit that to a ten-year-old?

We weren't made of money. I did need a break.
Our dog did go to live on a farm, for a while.
When I said, I'll think about it. I did.
You do know I was right about that girl.
Honestly, most of the time, I told you the truth.

Parenting is the most fulfilling, amazing, rewarding, wondrous job in the world. It is also the most challenging and confusing and deflating at times. We often go to bed at night wondering, 'Should I do more? Can I do better? Where did it go wrong?' With the noise of commercialism bellowing in our ears, this is a little reminder to go easy and keep it simple.

'Do not ask your children to strive'

William Martin

Do not ask your children
to strive for extraordinary lives.
Such striving may seem admirable,
but it is the way of foolishness.
Help them instead to find the wonder
and the marvel of an ordinary life.
Show them the joy of tasting
tomatoes, apples and pears.
Show them how to cry
when pets and people die.
Show them the infinite pleasure
in the touch of a hand.
And make the ordinary come alive for them.
The extraordinary will take care of itself.

Ever felt like the four walls were closing in on you? They say a change is as good as a rest. When I read this poem, I thought of those working/studying/cooking/ cleaning/parenting and everything else from home. It can be intense, and the juggle is real! This poem by Edna St. Vincent Millay captures that yearning to make a break for it with an interesting ending too.

Departure

Edna St. Vincent Millay

It's little I care what path I take,
And where it leads it's little I care,
But out of this house, lest my heart break,
I must go, and off somewhere!

It's little I know what's in my heart,
What's in my mind it's little I know,
But there's that in me must up and start,
And it's little I care where my feet go!

I wish I could walk for a day and a night,
And find me at dawn in a desolate place,
With never the rut of a road in sight,
Or the roof of a house, or the eyes of a face.

I wish I could walk till my blood should spout,
And drop me, never to stir again,
On a shore that is wide, for the tide is out,
And the weedy rocks are bare to the rain.

But dump or dock, where the path I take
Brings up, it's little enough I care,
And it's little I'd mind the fuss they'll make,
Huddled dead in a ditch somewhere.

'Is something the matter, dear,' she said,
'That you sit at your work so silently?'
'No, mother, no – 'twas a knot in my thread.
There goes the kettle – I'll make the tea.'

I read this poem on 'one of those days' and needed to read it. Jan Brierton is one of Ireland's most exciting new poets and the final stanza of 'But' is glorious.

But

Jan Brierton

The woman in me is exhausted,
The chef in me is out on strike.
The teacher in me has nothing to teach,
And the mother in me is in strife.

The housekeeper in me is dog tired,
The worker in me is off sick.
The student in me isn't listening,
And the wife in me thinks he's a dick
(Sometimes)

The peacemaker in me can't say sorry,
The friend in me – nothing to give.
The daughter in me pleads 'don't worry'
And the forgetter in me won't forgive.

The supporter in me has no chants left,
The juggler in me dropped the balls.
The reader in me can't finish a book,
And the caller in me dropped the call.

The cleaner in me threw the towel in,
The fashionista in me looks like crap.
The beauty in me, feels more like a beast,
And the gym bunny in me needs a nap.

The talker in me is gone silent,
The carer in me could care less.
The spender in me is insolvent,
And the organiser in me is a mess.

But.

The sharer in me is still sharing,
The thinker in me is still deep.
The lover in me, still has something to give.
And the dreamer in me's not asleep.

Sleep is a fundamental. Something we almost take for granted until we don't get enough of it! I always describe it as the pillar for our overall health and wellbeing and without it we don't eat, move, function properly. Sometimes we crave it so badly we almost beg the universe for it, as Keats does here.

To Sleep

John Keats

O soft embalmer of the still midnight,
    Shutting, with careful fingers and benign,
Our gloom-pleas'd eyes, embower'd from the light,
    Enshaded in forgetfulness divine;
O soothest Sleep! if so it please thee, close;
    In midst of this thine hymn, my willing eyes,
Or wait the amen, ere thy poppy throws
    Around my bed its lulling charities;
    Then save me, or the passed day will shine
Upon my pillow, breeding many woes;
    Save me from curious conscience, that still lords
Its strength for darkness, burrowing like a mole;
    Turn the key deftly in the oiled wards,
And seal the hushed casket of my soul.

For those who are 'domestically challenged' like myself...this one's for you!

Dust If You Must

Rose Milligan

Dust if you must, but wouldn't it be better
To paint a picture or write a letter,
Bake a cake or plant a seed,
Ponder the difference between want and need?

Dust if you must, but there's not much time,
With rivers to swim and mountains to climb,
Music to hear and books to read,
Friends to cherish and life to lead.

Dust if you must, but the world's out there,
With the sun in your eyes, the wind in your hair,
A flutter of snow, a shower of rain.
This day will not come around again.

Dust if you must, but bear in mind,
Old age will come and it's not kind.
And when you go – and go you must –
You, yourself, will make more dust.

'Love is no less practical than a coffee grinder or a safe spare tire'.

This line should be carved in stone as a reminder to us all. Self-love is the greatest gift you can give yourself.

The Word

Tony Hoagland

Down near the bottom
of the crossed-out list
of things you have to do today,

between 'green thread'
and 'broccoli' you find
that you have penciled 'sunlight.'

Resting on the page, the word
is beautiful, it touches you
as if you had a friend

and sunlight were a present
he had sent you from some place distant
as this morning – to cheer you up,

and to remind you that,
among your duties, pleasure
is a thing,

that also needs accomplishing
Do you remember?
that time and light are kinds

of love, and love
is no less practical
than a coffee grinder

or a safe spare tire?
Tomorrow you may be utterly
without a clue

but today you get a telegram,
from the heart in exile
proclaiming that the kingdom

still exists,
the king and queen alive,
still speaking to their children,

– to any one among them
who can find the time,
to sit out in the sun and listen.

The pressures of social media and society in general can be crippling. This beautiful piece by Becky Hemsley is a reminder to unplug, detach and give yourself time and space to simply breathe.

Breathe

Becky Hemsley

she sat at the back
and they said she was shy
she led from the front
and they hated her pride

they asked her advice
and then questioned her guidance
they branded her loud
then were shocked by her silence

when she shared no ambition
they said it was sad
so she told them her dreams
and they said she was mad

they told her they'd listen
then covered their ears
and gave her a hug
whilst they laughed at her fears

and she listened to all of it
thinking she should
be the girl they told her to be
best as she could

but one day she asked
what was best for herself
instead of trying
to please everyone else

so she walked to the forest
and stood with the trees
she heard the wind whisper
and dance with the leaves

and she spoke to the willow,
the elm and the pine
and she told them what she'd been told
time after time

she told them she never
felt nearly enough
she was either too little
or far, far too much

too loud or too quiet
too fierce or too weak
too wise or too foolish
too bold or too meek

then she found a small clearing
surrounded by firs
and she stopped and she heard
what the trees said to her

and she sat there for hours
not wanting to leave
for the forest said nothing...
it just let her breathe

For Mom.

My Mother

Ann Taylor

Who fed me from her gentle breast,
And hushed me in her arms to rest,
And on my cheek sweet kisses prest?
                My Mother.

When sleep forsook my open eye,
Who was it sung sweet lullaby,
And rocked me that I should not cry?
                My Mother.

Who sat and watched my infant head,
When sleeping in my cradle bed,
And tears of sweet affection shed?
                My Mother.

When pain and sickness made me cry,
Who gazed upon my heavy eye,
And wept for fear that I should die?
                My Mother.

Who ran to help me when I fell,
And would some pretty story tell,
Or kiss the part to make it well?
                My Mother.

Who taught my infant lips to pray,
To love God's holy word and day,
And walk in wisdom's pleasant way?
                    My Mother.

And can I ever cease to be
Affectionate and kind to thee,
Who was so very kind to me?
                    My Mother.

Oh, no! the thought I cannot bear,
And, if God please my life to spare,
I hope I shall reward thy care,
                    My Mother.

When thou art feeble, old and grey,
My healthy arm shall be thy stay,
And I will soothe thy pains away,
                    My Mother.

And when I see thee hang thy head,
'Twill be my turn to watch thy bed,
And tears of sweet affection shed,
                    My Mother.

I read this poem the night before a work trip abroad and it resonated so strongly with me. The level of planning involved to simply get out the door when you have smallies is no joke! I had all meals prepped, outfits laid out, instructions written and on the fridge, and of course I knew they were in safe hands yet STILL felt guilty leaving. This poem seemed to articulate those feelings.

Any Woman

Katharine Tynan

I am the pillars of the house;
The keystone of the arch am I.
Take me away, and roof and wall
Would fall to ruin me utterly.

I am the fire upon the hearth,
I am the light of the good sun,
I am the heat that warms the earth,
Which else were colder than a stone.

At me the children warm their hands;
I am their light of love alive.
Without me cold the hearthstone stands,
Nor could the precious children thrive.

I am the twist that holds together
The children in its sacred ring,
Their knot of love, from whose close tether
No lost child goes a-wandering.

I am the house from floor to roof,
I deck the walls, the board I spread;
I spin the curtains, warp and woof,
And shake the down to be their bed.

I am their wall against all danger,
Their door against the wind and snow,
Thou Whom a woman laid in a manger,
Take me not till the children grow!

After loss, we often feel guilt. This is a beautiful poem encouraging the mourner to begin to smile and live again.

Remember Me

Christina Rossetti

Remember me when I am gone away,
Gone far away into the silent land;
When you can no more hold me by the hand,
Nor I half turn to go, yet turning stay.
Remember me when no more day by day
You tell me of our future that you planned:
Only remember me; you understand
It will be late to counsel then or pray.
Yet if you should forget me for a while
And afterwards remember, do not grieve:
For if the darkness and corruption leave
A vestige of the thoughts that once I had,
Better by far you should forget and smile
Than that you should remember and be sad.

For my grandad, Chris Droney.

Grandad

Aoibhín Garrihy

I see you in us all
The best part of us all
The part of us that sees the good
Takes pride and stands up tall

The part of us that never settles
The part that does things right
The part of us up for the craic
That will dance and laugh all night

The part of us that listens
Loves stories and a chat
The part that worries, gives advice
And dons the carer's hat

The part that loves the simple things
But loves the nice things too
Sucky sweets, the motor car,
A well-kept lawn, a polished shoe

The part of us that lives for music
And all the joy it brings
The part that loves the get-together
As we tap along and sing

The part of us that loves family
The part that loves our home
The part that loves our place, our country
To travel and to roam

I see you in my Mom
My sisters and in me
I pray I'll see you in my girls
How lucky would they be?

So when we pause to think of you
Or they talk of your legacy
I'll only have to look around
You've passed it on, you see

For those missing a loved one...

Perhaps

Vera Brittain

Perhaps some day the sun will shine again,
　　And I shall see that still the skies are blue,
And feel once more I do not live in vain,
　　Although bereft of You.

Perhaps the golden meadows at my feet
　　Will make the sunny hours of Spring seem gay,
And I shall find the white May blossoms sweet,
　　Though You have passed away.

Perhaps the summer woods will shimmer bright,
　　And crimson roses once again be fair,
And autumn harvest fields a rich delight,
　　Although You are not there.

Perhaps some day I shall not shrink in pain
　　To see the passing of the dying year,
And listen to the Christmas songs again,
　　Although You cannot hear.

But, though kind Time may many joys renew,
　　There is one greatest joy I shall not know
Again, because my heart for loss of You
　　Was broken, long ago.

A 'glass half full' poem if ever needed. I just love Brontë's hope and optimism throughout this piece.

Life

Charlotte Brontë

Life, believe, is not a dream
    So dark as sages say;
Oft a little morning rain
    Foretells a pleasant day.
Sometimes there are clouds of gloom,
    But these are transient all;
If the shower will make the roses bloom,
    Oh, why lament its fall?
        Rapidly, merrily,
    Life's sunny hours flit by,
        Gratefully, cheerily,
    Enjoy them as they fly!

What though Death at times steps in,
    And calls our best away?
What though sorrow seems to win,
    O'er hope, a heavy sway?
Yet Hope again elastic springs,
    Unconquered, though she fell;
Still buoyant are her golden wings,
    Still strong to bear us well.
        Manfully, fearlessly,
    The day of trial bear,
        For gloriously, victoriously,
    Can courage quell despair!

I loved this poem even before knowing Amelia Earhart's story. She was the first woman to fly solo across the Atlantic Ocean, in 1932.

Courage

Amelia Earhart

Courage is the price that Life exacts for granting
   peace.

The soul that knows it not knows no release
From little things:

Knows not the livid loneliness of fear,
Nor mountain heights where bitter joy can hear
The sound of wings.

How can life grant us boon of living, compensate
For dull gray ugliness and pregnant hate
Unless we dare

The soul's dominion? Each time we make a choice,
   we pay
With courage to behold the resistless day,
And count it fair.

No good deed or act of kindness, however small, is ever in vain.

If I Can Stop One Heart from Breaking

Emily Dickinson

If I can stop one heart
from breaking,
I shall not live in vain;

If I can ease one life the aching,
Or cool one pain,

Or help one fainting robin
Unto his nest again,

I shall not live in vain.

In an age of anxiety, insomnia, stress…how wonderful to end the day utterly fulfilled and totally content.

Happy the Man

John Dryden

Happy the man, and happy he alone,
    He who can call today his own:
    He who, secure within, can say,
Tomorrow do thy worst, for I have lived today.
    Be fair or foul or rain or shine
The joys I have possessed, in spite of fate, are mine.
Not Heaven itself upon the past has power,
But what has been, has been, and I have had my hour.

It's OK not to be OK...a beautiful poem about self-compassion.

The Mountain

Laura Ding-Edwards

If the mountain seems too big today
then climb a hill instead.
If the morning brings you sadness
it's ok to stay in bed.
If the day ahead weighs heavy
and your plans feel like a curse,
there's no shame in rearranging,
don't make yourself feel worse.
If a shower stings like needles
and a bath feels like you'll drown,
if you haven't washed your hair for days,
don't throw away your crown.
A day is not a lifetime
a rest is not defeat,
don't think of it as failure,
just a quiet, kind retreat.
It's ok to take a moment
from an anxious, fractured mind,
the world will not stop turning
while you get realigned.
The mountain will still be there
when you want to try again,
you can climb it in your own time,
just love yourself til then.

Dating back to the 1800s, there are lines from this poem that will be familiar to many. It's a reminder of our innate ability to dream, to believe and to achieve.

From **The Music-Makers**

Arthur O'Shaughnessy

We are the music-makers,
    And we are the dreamers of dreams,
Wandering by lone sea-breakers,
    And sitting by desolate streams;
World-losers and world-forsakers,
    On whom the pale moon gleams;
Yet we are the movers and shakers
    Of the world for ever, it seems.

With wonderful deathless ditties
We build up the world's great cities,
    And out of a fabulous story
    We fashion an empire's glory:
One man with a dream, at pleasure,
    Shall go forth and conquer a crown;
And three with a new song's measure
    Can trample an empire down.

We, in the ages lying
    In the buried past of the earth,
Built Ninevah with our sighing,
    And Babel itself with our mirth;
And o'erthrew them with prophesying
    To the old of the new world's worth;
For each age is a dream that is dying,
    Or one that is coming to birth.

Kindness matters.

Count That Day Lost

George Eliot

If you sit down at set of sun
And count the acts that you have done,
And, counting, find
One self-denying deed, one word
That eased the heart of him who heard,
One glance most kind
That fell like sunshine where it went –
Then you may count that day well spent.

But if, through all the livelong day,
You've cheered no heart, by yea or nay –
If, through it all
You've nothing done that you can trace
That brought the sunshine to one face –
No act most small
That helped some soul and nothing cost –
Then count that day as worse than lost.

This is one I remember fondly from schooldays. I loved it even as a teenager. I've always been a bit of a risk-taker so taking the road 'less travelled by' has always appealed to me. I think it's a lovely reminder to weigh things up beforehand but ultimately, go with your gut instinct. It generally serves us well.

The Road Not Taken

Robert Frost

Two roads diverged in a yellow wood,
And sorry I could not travel both
And be one traveler, long I stood
And looked down one as far as I could
To where it bent in the undergrowth;

Then took the other, as just as fair,
And having perhaps the better claim,
Because it was grassy and wanted wear;
Though as for that the passing there
Had worn them really about the same,

And both that morning equally lay
In leaves no step had trodden black.
Oh, I kept the first for another day!
Yet knowing how way leads on to way,
I doubted if I should ever come back.

I shall be telling this with a sigh
Somewhere ages and ages hence:
Two roads diverged in a wood, and I –
I took the one less traveled by,
And that has made all the difference.

Positive self-talk can be a game changer so here's a little reminder to ignore (or take with a pinch of salt) the voice of your inner critic.

Thinking

Walter D. Wintle

If you think you are beaten, you are;
  If you think you dare not, you don't.
If you'd like to win, but think you can't,
  It is almost a cinch you won't.

If you think you'll lose, you're lost,
  For out in the world we find
Success begins with a fellow's will —
  It's all in the state of mind.

If you think you're outclassed, you are;
  You've got to think high to rise;
You've got to be sure of yourself before
  You can ever win a prize.

Life's battles don't always go
  To the stronger or faster man;
But soon or late the man who wins,
  Is the man who thinks he can.

A hugely popular and inspirational poem. Dating back to the 1800s, 'If' continues to win the hearts of many.

If –

Rudyard Kipling

If you can keep your head when all about you
    Are losing theirs and blaming it on you;
If you can trust yourself when all men doubt you,
    But make allowance for their doubting too;
If you can wait and not be tired by waiting,
    Or being lied about, don't deal in lies,
Or being hated, don't give way to hating,
    And yet don't look too good, nor talk too wise;

If you can dream – and not make dreams your master;
    If you can think – and not make thoughts your aim,
If you can meet with Triumph and Disaster
    And treat those two impostors just the same;
If you can bear to hear the truth you've spoken
    Twisted by knaves to make a trap for fools,
Or watch the things you gave your life to, broken,
    And stoop and build 'em up with worn-out tools;

If you can make one heap of all your winnings
    And risk it on one turn of pitch-and-toss,
And lose, and start again at your beginnings
    And never breathe a word about your loss;
If you can force your heart and nerve and sinew
    To serve your turn long after they are gone,
And so hold on when there is nothing in you
    Except the Will which says to them: 'Hold on!'

If you can talk with crowds and keep your virtue,
    Or walk with Kings – nor lose the common touch,
If neither foes nor loving friends can hurt you,
    If all men count with you, but none too much;
If you can fill the unforgiving minute
    With sixty seconds' worth of distance run,
Yours is the Earth and everything that's in it,
    And – which is more – you'll be a Man, my son!

I think this is the ultimate mirror 'pep talk'. When the chips are down, we discover what it is we are truly made of. I believe it was one of Nelson Mandela's favourites too and he recited it on Robben Island.

Invictus

W.E. Henley

Out of the night that covers me,
   Black as the pit from pole to pole,
I thank whatever gods may be
   For my unconquerable soul.

In the fell clutch of circumstance
   I have not winced nor cried aloud.
Under the bludgeonings of chance
   My head is bloody, but unbowed.

Beyond this place of wrath and tears
   Looms but the Horror of the shade,
And yet the menace of the years
   Finds and shall find me unafraid.

It matters not how strait the gate,
   How charged with punishments the scroll,
I am the master of my fate,
   I am the captain of my soul.

For anyone prepared to lift their head above the parapet, who has the courage to step into the ring, whatever form that takes, this piece is for you (and remember, it's easy to comment from the sidelines!).

The Man in the Arena

Theodore Roosevelt

It is not the critic who counts; not the man who
points out how the strong man stumbles, or where
the doer of deeds could have done them better.

The credit belongs to the man who is actually
in the arena, whose face is marred by dust and sweat
and blood; who strives valiantly; who errs, who comes
short again and again, because there is no effort
without error and shortcoming; but who does actually
strive to do the deeds; who knows great enthusiasms,
the great devotions; who spends himself in a worthy
cause; who at the best knows in the end the triumph
of high achievement, and who at the worst, if he
fails, at least fails while daring greatly, so that his
place shall never be with those cold and timid
souls who neither know victory nor defeat.

My mom would often say, 'It's nice to be important but it's far more important to be nice.' This is a wonderful reminder that we are all simply 'passing through' and so, adopting a humble approach is the way to go. The simplicity of the analogy is what I really love about this poem.

Indispensable Man

Saxon White Kessinger

Sometime when you're feeling important;
Sometime when your ego's in bloom
Sometime when you take it for granted
You're the best qualified in the room,

Sometime when you feel that your going
Would leave an unfillable hole,
Just follow these simple instructions
And see how they humble your soul;

Take a bucket and fill it with water,
Put your hand in it up to the wrist,
Pull it out and the hole that's remaining
Is a measure of how you'll be missed.

You can splash all you wish when you enter,
You may stir up the water galore,
But stop and you'll find that in no time
It looks quite the same as before.

The moral of this quaint example
Is do just the best that you can,
Be proud of yourself but remember,
There's no indispensable man.

A firm favourite of my mom's – 'Desiderata'. It's packed with real gems to live by and each time you read it a new line will jump out and resonate. It's a great one to revisit time and time again.

Desiderata

Max Ehrmann

Go placidly amid the noise and the haste, and remember what peace there may be in silence. As far as possible, without surrender, be on good terms with all persons.

Speak your truth quietly and clearly; and listen to others, even to the dull and the ignorant; they too have their story.

Avoid loud and aggressive persons; they are vexatious to the spirit. If you compare yourself with others, you may become vain or bitter, for always there will be greater and lesser persons than yourself.

Enjoy your achievements as well as your plans. Keep interested in your own career, however humble; it is a real possession in the changing fortunes of time.

Exercise caution in your business affairs, for the world is full of trickery. But let this not blind you to what virtue there is; many persons strive for high ideals, and everywhere life is full of heroism.

Be yourself. Especially, do not feign affection. Neither be cynical about love; for in the face of all aridity and disenchantment, it is as perennial as the grass.

Take kindly the counsel of the years, gracefully surrendering the things of youth.

Nurture strength of spirit to shield you in sudden misfortune. But do not distress yourself with dark imaginings. Many fears are born of fatigue and loneliness.

Beyond a wholesome discipline, be gentle with yourself. You are a child of the universe no less than the trees and the stars; you have a right to be here.

And whether or not it is clear to you, no doubt the universe is unfolding as it should. Therefore be at peace with God, whatever you conceive Him to be. And whatever your labors and aspirations, in the noisy confusion of life, keep peace in your soul. With all its sham, drudgery and broken dreams, it is still a beautiful world. Be cheerful. Strive to be happy.

The title of this poem is a mantra for life. Everything is temporary.

This, Too, Shall Pass Away

Lanta Wilson Smith

When some great sorrow, like a mighty river,
Flows through your life with peace-destroying power,
And dearest things are swept from sight forever,
Say to your heart each trying hour:
'This, too, shall pass away.'

When ceaseless toil has hushed your song of
    gladness,
And you have grown almost too tired to pray,
Let this truth banish from your heart its sadness,
And ease the burdens of each trying day:
'This, too, shall pass away.'

When fortune smiles, and, full of mirth and pleasure,
The days are flitting by without a care,
Lest you should rest with only earthly treasure,
Let these few words their fullest import bear:
'This, too, shall pass away.'

When earnest labor brings you fame and glory,
And all earth's noblest ones upon you smile,
Remember that life's longest, grandest story
Fills but a moment in earth's little while:
'This, too, shall pass away.'

Our natural instinct is to fight what we fear but often when we reframe our mindset and arrive at a place of acceptance it can make all the difference.

Allow

Danna Faulds

There is no controlling life.
Try corralling a lightning bolt,
containing a tornado. Dam a
stream, and it will create a new
channel. Resist, and the tide
will sweep you off your feet.
Allow, and grace will carry
you to higher ground. The only
safety lies in letting it all in –
the wild with the weak; fear,
fantasies, failures and success.
When loss rips off the doors of
the heart, or sadness veils your
vision with despair, practice
becomes simply bearing the truth.
In the choice to let go of your
known way of being, the whole
world is revealed to your new eyes.

This reminds me of one of my favourite quotes by Erin Hanson, 'And you ask, what if I fall? Oh but my darling, what if you fly?'

That risk is worth taking. If you never try, you'll never know.

Come to the Edge

Christopher Logue

Come to the edge.
We might fall.
Come to the edge.
It's too high!
COME TO THE EDGE!
And they came,
And he pushed,
And they flew.

Index of First Lines

Acknowledgements

The editor and publisher gratefully acknowledge permission to reproduce the following copyright poems in this book:

Wendell Berry: Wendell Berry, 'The Peace of Wild Things' from *New Collected Poems*. Copyright © 2012 by Wendell Berry. Reprinted with the permission of The Permissions Company, LLC on behalf of Counterpoint Press, counterpointpress.com.

Denise Blake: 'And They All Lived Happily' by Denise Blake from 'Invocation', Revival Press – Limerick Writers Centre © 2018.

Jan Brierton: 'But' a new poem by Jan Brierton © 2022 reproduced by kind permission of Jan Brierton.

Vera Brittain: Vera Brittain's 'Perhaps' is reproduced by permission of Mark Bostridge and T.J. Brittain-Catlin, Literary Executors for the Estate of Vera Brittain 1970.

Sean Brophy: 'Friendship' by Sean Brophy from *The Awakening and Other Poems*, Rainsford Press, 1992.

About the Author

Aoibhín Garrihy is an actress, voiceover artist, entrepreneur and social media influencer. Having graduated with a BA in Acting Studies at Trinity College Dublin in 2009, she became well known for her work in TV dramas such as Fair City, The Fall and on stage productions at The Gate Theatre. In recent years she co-founded renowned lifestyle and wellness brand BEO. She lives in Co Clare with her husband John and three young daughters.